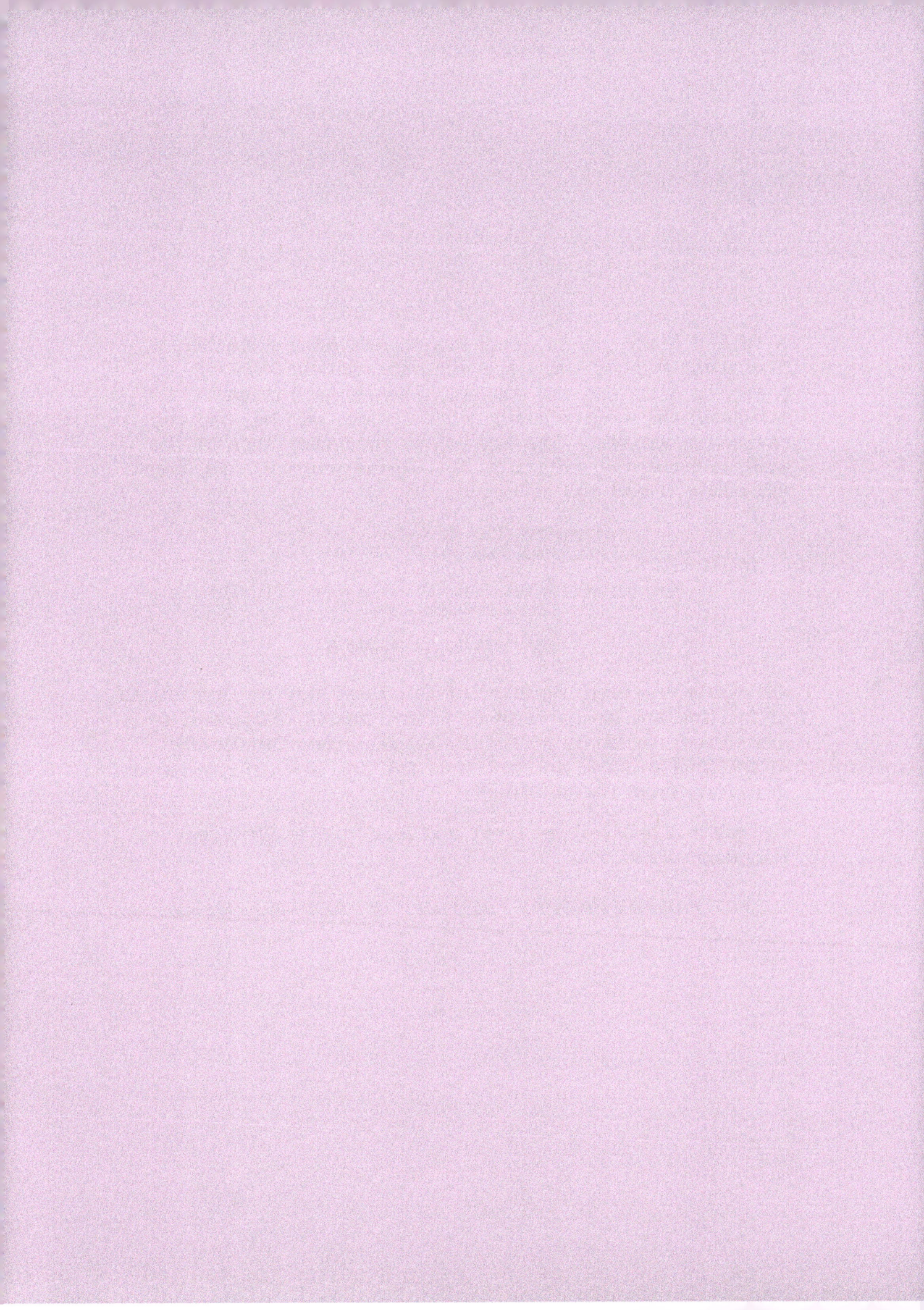

A special thank you to Jordi Moore, our editor-in-chief. She spent endless hours providing her guidance, insight, provoking questions and support. She co-facilitated conversations in determining word choice, editing, and the revision processes. She has valued the importance of the work in supporting others on their grief journey. She is an incredible friend and colleague.

Copyright © 2024 by Kaylene Ashbridge
Illustrations Copyright © 2024 Lynn Byrn

First published in the United States of America in 2024
by Sun Baked Studio

ISBN: 979-8-218-43798-5

For more support about grief and loss, please visit our Facebook group page:

"Families Grieving Together For Hope and Healing"

This story is based on a real experience in the author's backyard. A special thank you to my friend John, who first noticed the nest being built on his visit with us.

Perched in Our Heart

Author: Kaylene Ashbridge

Illustrator: Lynn Byrn

A Family Read-Aloud Book
About Loss and Healing

Mama Hummingbird was building her nest
in the heart-shaped wind chime hanging on
a family's back porch.

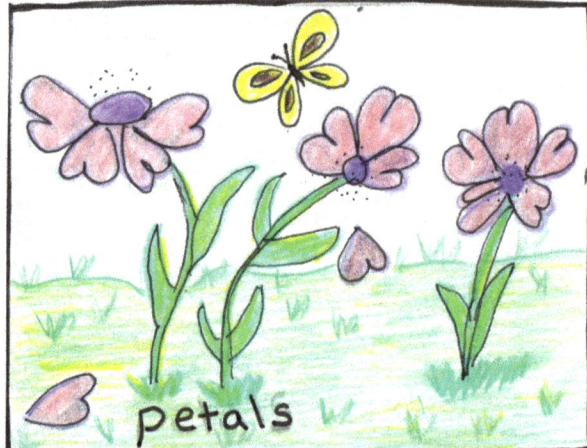

She gathered twigs, leaves, petals, and feathers carefully creating a cozy spot for her eggs.

"Come quick, a hummingbird is building a nest,"
whispered Johnny. See her? She moves so fast!"

His older brother, Justin, squeezed in by
the window to get a better look.

Justin said, "I've been reading about hummingbirds.

Did you know they can fly upside down and backwards?"

"It looks like Mama Hummingbird has chosen our special wind chime for her home. Should we give our new guest a name?" asked Dad. "She's so quick. I think Zips would be a great name!" exclaimed Mom.

When Grandpa came over the next day, the boys couldn't wait to show him the nest.

He brought out a ladder so they could get a better look.

"Don't get too close," warned Grandpa. Zips hovered nearby as the boys peered in to discover two tiny eggs.

For the next two weeks, Zips rotated her body, keeping her eggs warm. She only left the nest to get herself a quick sip of nectar.

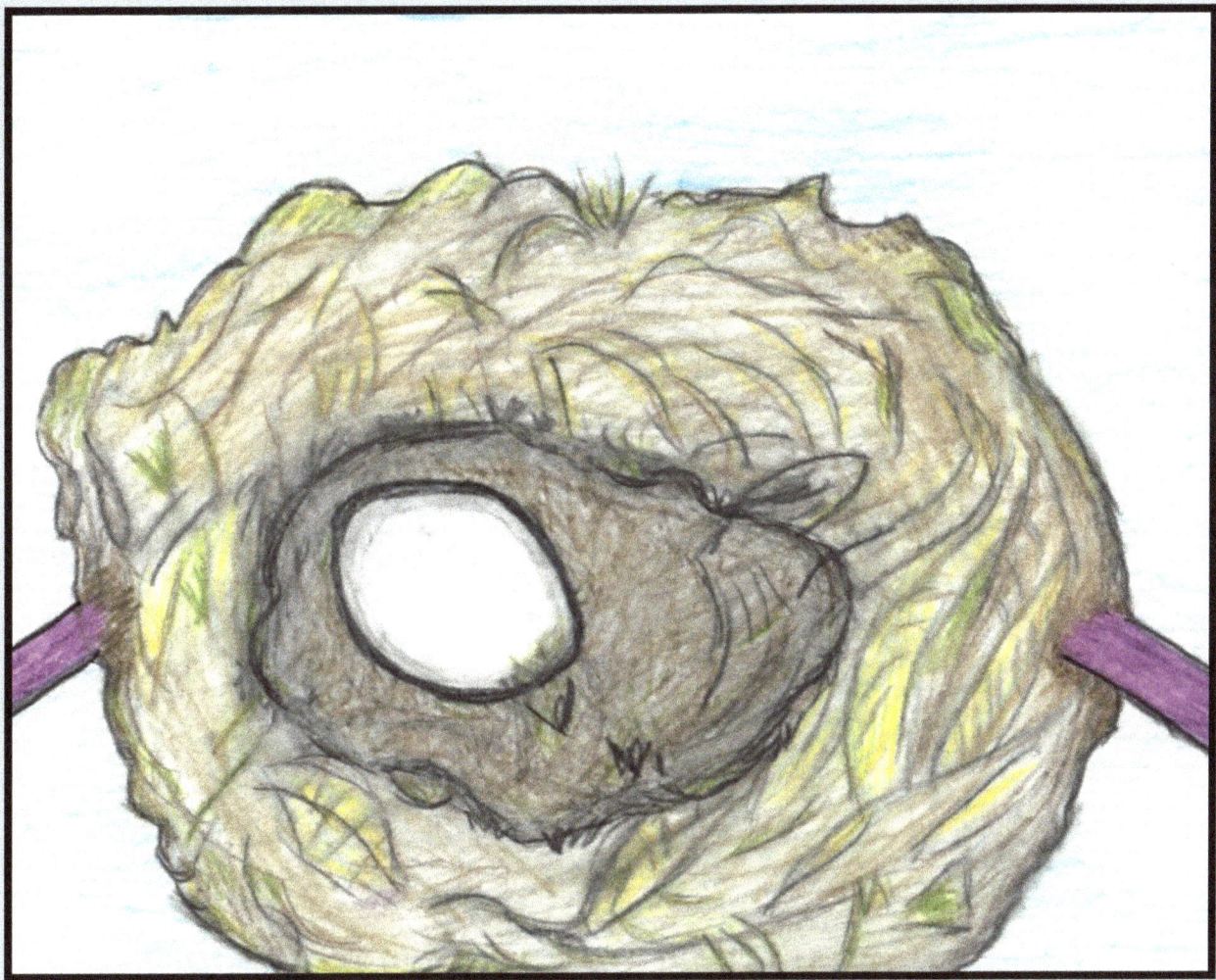

Each morning the boys checked on the nest, but today, there was only one egg. They noticed some broken shells on the ground. "Remember, dad told us not all eggs hatch. I sure hope the other one survives!" said Justin.

At last the day came when Justin noticed a tiny head peeking out from the nest. The baby's beak was open, letting Zips know it was ready to eat. That reminded him of his baby sister Jewels when she was hungry. Since her death, she was always on his mind.

Zips left her nest often, gathering nectar to feed her tiny baby. The family enjoyed watching her flitter from the nest to the flowers and back. "She is such a good mother!" said Johnny.

"The baby sure has a lot of attitude! Let's name her Sassy," said Justin.

Yet there were some quiet moments when Zips and Sassy would sit together, ever so still. It seemed that they loved their time together, gazing out from their nest at the flowers in the family's backyard.

Baby hummingbirds only have three weeks before leaving their nest and flying off on their own. Johnny felt sad that Sassy would not be a part of their family much longer. He didn't want things to change...

but change **is** a part of life.

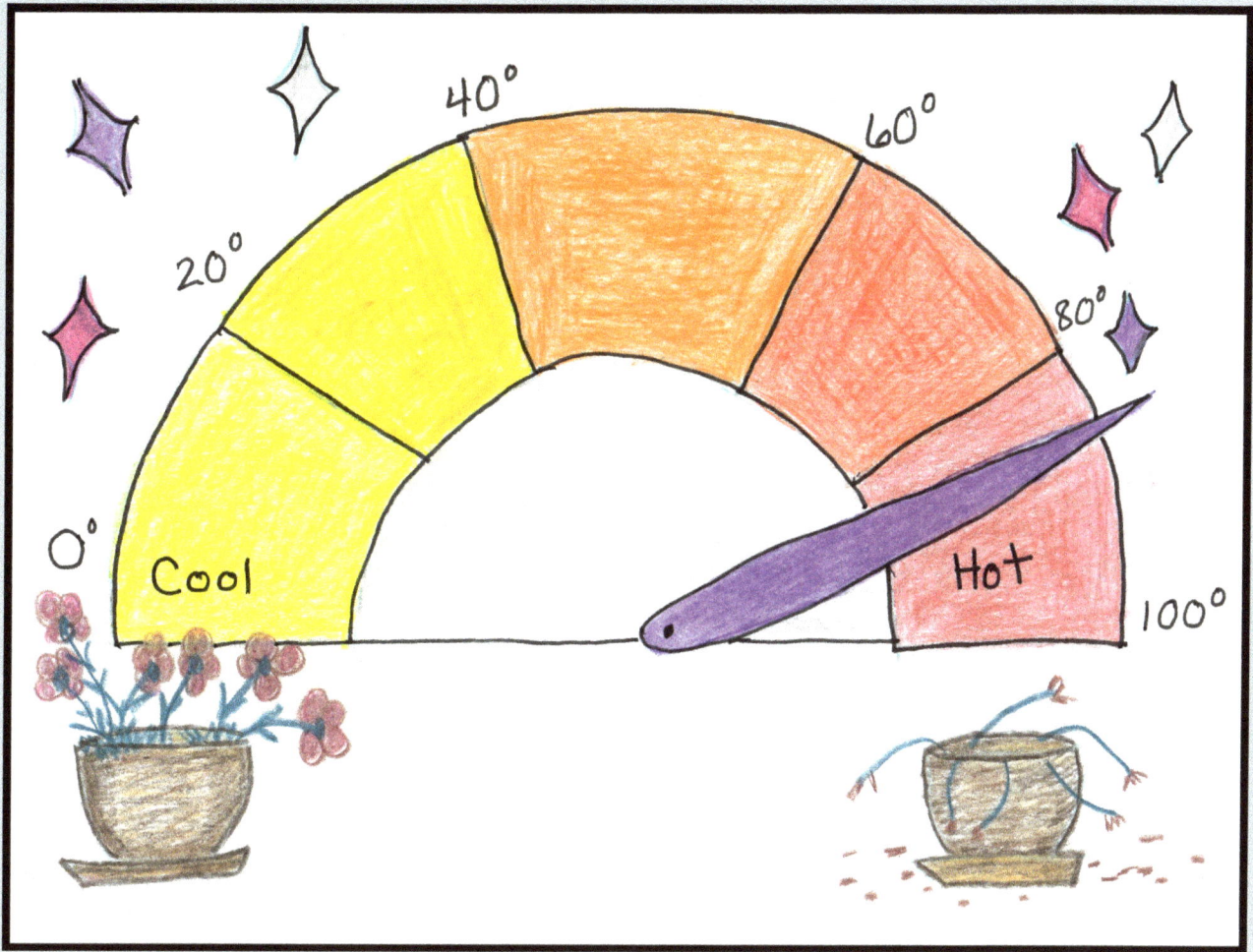

Summer came quickly in the Arizona desert. The days were getting hotter and hotter and the sun was intense.

It was hard for Zips to get enough nectar from the drying plants.

Zips spent most of her days looking for food. The high temperatures were causing her to slow down. She was growing weary.

The scorching heat continued and
Sassy was without enough
nourishment to survive.

Her heart
stopped
beating.

She died. . .
bringing an overwhelming sadness
to the whole family. This feeling
was familiar to them. . .
but
never talked about.

"Why did Sassy have to die?" cried Johnny.

Justin began to cry.
"Why did baby Jewels have to die?"

With tears in her eyes, mom shared, "It's hard to understand. We all knew Jewels' heart wasn't strong. The doctors tried to help her, but she became weak like Sassy. She couldn't recover. I've been so overwhelmed. It's been hard for me to talk about it with you."

"We've all been feeling so sad," whispered Dad. "It seems like our little bird family just might help us talk about Jewels again."

Grandpa was quiet for a moment, then said, "Both Sassy and Jewels brought us so much happiness even if it was for a very short time. It is important to cherish the memories of those we love just like we remember Grandma."

"Our friends and family got together for Jewels. Let's do the same for Sassy," said Justin. The family agreed to gather for a special memorial.

Sassy was to be buried by the heart-shaped wind chime, a gift the family had received at Jewels' memorial. Each of them shared a memory they had of their baby hummingbird. Then talked about a special moment they each had with baby Jewels.

Zips hovered overhead, resting a moment on the heart-shaped chime. Looking up, Dad reflected, "I think Zips and Sassy helped us recognize our own unspoken grief for Jewels. We need to support each other and take time to mourn.

"Zips, you and Sassy will forever be perched in our hearts!"

It has been said that hummingbirds and other living creatures come to those who need hope, healing, and encouragement.

This story ends but the family's grief journey begins as they start to mourn and share their feelings and questions with each other. When Sassy died, it brought a shared connection for the whole family to be able to talk about the loss of their sister/daughter/granddaughter. Everyone's journey is unique. Wherever you are in yours, we encourage you to share your story through our Facebook community: "Families Grieving Together for Hope and Healing."

Dedicated to:
Mayzie Claire Humphrey
(Amazing Mayzie)

This story is dedicated to Mayzie, a precious little girl, strong in spirit and born medically fragile. Hummingbirds have supported her family and others in their grief journey. Her mom shared, "Hummingbirds tend to visit us at the most unexpected times with encounters feeling so personal and intimate that we can't help but think that our Mayzie sent them to remind us of her presence."

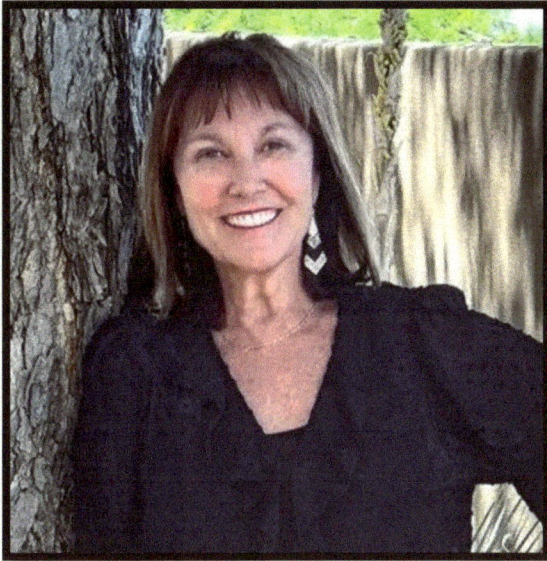

Meet the Author

Kaylene Ashbridge is a retired educator who served as a teacher, counselor, and principal. She is currently working as a School Bereavement Liaison and Group Night Coordinator/Specialist at Billy's Place, a non-profit supporting grieving children. She lives in Phoenix, Arizona with her husband Drew and their Australian Labradoodle Abby. Her son Justin, lives in Mesa, Arizona. She is passionate about helping families as they navigate their profound feelings of loss and learn to communicate and mourn together.

Meet the Illustrator

Lynn Byrn is a Mixed Media Artist experimenting with Collage, from Glendale, Arizona, Founder of Sun Baked Studio in 2022 named after the process of drying many layers of collage in the Arizona sun. She is a first-time illustrator. Her art is inspired by real events. Touched by the theme of hope in this family's story, the illustrations reflect actual people, locations and experiences.

As you mourn...

Navigating loss is a challenging journey. It can be hard to communicate all the big feelings one experiences when a family member dies. Grief is what we feel on the inside, and mourning is the individual way we can express those feelings outwardly.

Each member will have his/her own way of grieving but it is important to mourn as individuals and together as a family. Children mimic what their parents do. There is great value in revealing one's feelings through words, play, art, and commemorative activities.

As in the story, the family participated in a memorial service for the baby bird and their special person Jewels. Such experiences provide a space for each family member to acknowledge their loss and help create a home that support both the happy and sad times.

Ideas for Discussing Grief with Your Children/Family

- Talk about death in daily experiences as a natural part of the life cycle. All living things die. Normalizing death in nature helps children cope with relational losses.
- Look for conversations related to death/loss and bring it up by using the situation as a teachable moment.
- Create an open environment where family members may share their "big feelings" like sadness, guilt, and anger to support healthy emotional development.
- Talk about a memory you have of...
- Share something you love about ...
- Since your loss, what are same changes that have happened since your "special person" has died?
- What brings you comfort when you have big emotions?

Be there. .

Loss comes in many forms: miscarriage, incarceration, divorce, losing a child, a parent, a family member, a friend, an acquaintance, a pet...

When someone has experienced a loss, be present and available. Acknowledging someone's grief is so important and it isn't something to "just get over." Sometimes that can simply mean "being there."

May this book and the Facebook group bring a sense of community and understanding. Seeking assistance from local grief agencies through counseling and peer support could guide those who are grieving and mourning. Additional resources are available at familiesgrievingtogether.com.

The National Alliance for Children's Grief (NACG) is a valuable national organization dedicated to supporting children and their families who are grieving.

Visit nacg.org to locate centers/camps near you.